Backyard Birdfeeding

Backyard Birdfeeding

John F. Gardner

STACKPOLE
BOOKS

Published by
STACKPOLE BOOKS
5067 Ritter Road
Mechanicsburg, PA 17055

Printed in the United States of America

10 9 8 7 6 5 4 3 2 1

First edition

Cover design by Tracy Patterson
Various illustrations courtesy of Duncraft, Inc.

Library of Congress Cataloging-in-Publication Data

Gardner, John F.
    Backyard birdfeeding / John F. Gardner. — 1st ed.
        p.   cm.
    ISBN 0-8117-2503-0 (pb)
    1. Bird feeders. 2. Birds—Feeding and
feeds. 3. Bird attracting. I. Title.
QL676.5.G365   1996
598—dc20   95-44223
                                            CIP

To Ed Manners, who took me on my first bird walk and taught me about hawks at Cape May, about shorebirds along the Delaware River, about owls in the pine woods of Deptford, about holly trees, and about nature's ways.

He introduced me to Haines and Potter and the old eggers, and to many birders at the Delaware Valley Ornithological Society. It was Ed who introduced me to Dorothy Poole, who taught me that nature and education were compatible and important. She had a sense of companionship with life out-of-doors and an abiding love of nature.

I remember the lessons, the walks, and the fun. They remain with me even today.

Contents

Introduction

More and more people are discovering the pleasures of backyard birdfeeding. It's fun to watch the birds come and go; to note the fascinating variety of sizes, shapes, and colors; and to observe how they eat, preen, and care for their young. It's a special treat to listen to their varied and delightful songs.

Backyard birdfeeding has become so popular in recent years that today about one fourth of American families feed wild birds. This book will help you get started so you too can enjoy avian visitors to your backyard.

Feeding birds is educational as well as enjoyable. At your feeder you'll see a variety of territorial, courtship, and migratory behavior. You may even attract one or two birds with some peculiar traits. For example, I once saw a cartoon showing a bird tapping on the window when the feeder was empty. Well, that doesn't just happen in cartoons! I met a woman who told me that a blue jay would tap on her window when the feeder was low on seed. So don't be surprised if this happens to you.

Some people worry that birdfeeding will cause birds to depend too much on an "artificial" food source, but most professional and

Birch

Through birdfeeding, many people have learned to appreciate nature's systems and cycles.

A schoolyard birdfeeding station can add a great deal to classroom subjects, from science and geography to ecology and even math.

amateur ornithologists agree that this isn't the case. Birds will continue to forage in the woods, fields, yards, gardens, and meadows for natural foods and rely on a birdfeeder only for supplemental food.

There are times, however, when feeders become especially important. For example, when the ground is covered with snow and ice, natural foods are frozen and therefore inaccessible. The birdfeeding station then becomes the birds' primary food source. Birds may also rely on a feeder after a long winter, when natural foods are scarce. Sometimes spring migrating birds get caught in a cold snap or late winter storm and can't find natural food. Birdfeeding stations are also vital after natural disasters, such as hurricanes or tornadoes, when natural foods are suddenly stripped away. In such cases the native birds must depart quickly for better natural habitat or depend almost entirely on birdfeeders.

People also benefit from feeding birds. For many, young and old alike—especially those who are homebound—the backyard birdfeeder is their only connection with the natural world. By observing birds at the feeder, people learn to appreciate nature, its systems and cycles. They become familiar with daily natural events surrounding them. The blue of a jay, the gray of the junco, the silhouette of a winter tree, the new buds of spring, and the music of the bird chorus all add to their understanding and enjoyment of nature—and of life.

If you've fed birds before, you already know that birdfeeding is enjoyable, educational, and beneficial. If you've picked up this book to learn how to get started, you'll soon find companionship with life out-of-doors. You will be enriched by the feeder in your yard, and birdfeeding will become a fun-filled, lifelong hobby.

Good birding.

The Backyard Feeder

Birdfeeding is a hobby you can enjoy all year. If you keep your feeder up year-round, you will attract a wide variety of birds. You will also be giving them a regular source of food that won't be affected by variations in the natural food supply.

Many people consider autumn to be the best time to set up a feeding station because birds are attracted to feeders as the weather turns harsh. Birds will visit feeders during all seasons, though, so you can start at any time of year.

In the fall, migrating birds fill up at the feeder to prepare for their long flights. In the winter, when natural food supplies are scarce, birds need feeders to provide a quick source of energy to help them stay warm and survive in the cold. In the spring, as the weather gets warmer, birds will visit feeders as they wait for natural foods to become more abundant. In summer, hummingbirds and orioles visit nectar feeders, and parents of various species will bring their young to the feeder. Summer is also the best time to attract robins, scarlet tanagers, and catbirds by providing fruit.

If you don't want to feed the birds year-round, at least keep the feeder stocked during

The spring is the most critical time for birds; they are active, and natural foods are in short supply.

the early spring. Early spring can be very stressful for birds, so don't take a feeder down until the leaves are fully out on the trees. In the fall, plants are heavy with ripened berries, seeds, and fruits, and birds have plenty of natural food in the fields and woods. Five months later most of that food is gone—fruits and seeds are just buds, and nuts and berries are still weeks away.

Birds get up very early in the morning, usually before sunrise, and the first thing they do is look for food. To ensure that there is plenty of food for the birds first thing in the morning, fill your feeder in the late evening. If a lot of birds visit your feeder, you might want to fill it in the early afternoon as well, as birds need to eat before they go to sleep. A full feeder in the afternoon gives the birds the opportunity to find sufficient food before nightfall. By keeping your feeder full you'll also ensure yourself a wide variety of birds to watch.

Sometimes changes in the local environment will limit the natural food supplies that birds depend on. These changes can be permanent, as when a field is paved as a parking lot, or temporary, as when a hurricane makes landfall and washes away the food supply. A late winter or early spring ice storm can lock up natural food supplies until a thaw.

To be a real friend to the birds that you feed, keep an eye on local conditions and change your feeding patterns accordingly. Watch the birds, too. You need to observe birds only a short time to discover how local conditions affect their lives.

The key to successful feeding is to keep in

If you feed a lot of birds, fill your feeder in the early afternoon and again before dark.

mind that birds tend to stay in an area where
there is an abundance of food, shelter, nesting
sites, and water. If you provide these things, you
will attract many fascinating birds.

*There are many different
kinds of commercially made
feeders and feeds available
today. A satellite feeder
filled with sunflower seeds
is a popular combination.*

Attracting Birds to Your Backyard

Setting up a backyard feeding station is an easy way to attract many fascinating birds to your garden or backyard. Birds' needs are simple—food, water, shelter, and nesting sites. By providing these necessities you can enjoy backyard birds in abundance.

The secret to attracting birds to your yard lies in the answers to these four questions:

What birds do you want to attract?

What type of habitat do they need?

What feeders do they use?

What natural foods do they eat?

Once you determine these things, you can design a feeding station just right for your area.

Cornell University's Project Feeder Watch reports that the most common backyard feeder bird in the United States is the dark-eyed junco.

Common Feeder Birds

The types of birds you can attract to your home will depend largely on where you live. Brief descriptions are given here for a number of common feeder birds you may be able to attract to your backyard. For more detailed information, consult a field guide.

Dark-eyed Junco. This is probably the most common feeder bird in the United States. The male has a dark gray body and a white breast. The female is brown. Watch for the white outer

Dark-eyed Junco

American Goldfinch

Blue Jay

House Finch

Mourning Dove

Downy Woodpecker

tail feathers as the bird flies. Dark-eyed juncos are sometimes called "snow birds." Juncos eat a variety of weed seeds.

American Goldfinch. Many people call this bird the "wild canary" because if its yellow color during breeding season. (It turns a dull brownish-green in the winter.) Goldfinches are found at niger feeders in flocks of twenty or more all year-round.

Blue Jay. A member of the crow family, the blue jay is an eastern bird but has relatives in the West: the stellar's jay and the scrub jay. The blue jay's favorite food is acorns, but it loves peanuts in the shell.

House Finch. This is a Western species. It escaped to the wild from New York City pet stores in the 1940s and populations rapidly spread back to the West. It feeds at a niger feeder and often nests in door wreaths.

Mourning Dove. A regular visitor to backyard feeding stations—often in flocks of twenty or more—the mourning dove loves millet of any kind.

Downy Woodpecker. Often confused with the hairy woodpecker, this is the smallest woodpecker species. The male has a red spot on the back of its head. At the feeder it will eat suet, peanuts, nutmeats, and corn.

Northern Cardinal. This is the most popular backyard bird in the East. Its favorite food is hulled sunflowers; it will eat whole corn if sunflower seed is not available.

House Sparrow. This is a common, if not always welcome, backyard bird. Introduced from Europe in the mid-1880s, the house sparrow is not fond of swinging feeders, which might help you discourage them from feeding at your station.

Black-capped Chickadee. The second most popular backyard bird, the black-capped chickadee will sometimes take food from your hand. They like sunflowers, peanuts, nutmeats, and suet.

European Starling. This species, which was also introduced from Europe in the mid-1880s, is especially fond of baked goods. Separate feeders filled with rolls, doughnuts, bread, or dry dog food will keep them away from the main feeding station.

White-breasted Nuthatch. This species is often called the "upside-down bird" because of its habit of walking down tree trunks head-first. It is a regular visitor to suet feeders in the winter.

American Robin. This species will visit backyard feeders if you put out berries—or small seeds or crumbs if berries are in short supply.

Tufted Titmouse. This is a small, blue-gray bird with large eyes and a white breast and tuft. It lives in the East; plain titmice live in the West.

Northern Cardinal

House Sparrow

Black-capped Chickadee

European Starling

White-breasted Nuthatch

American Robin

Tufted titmice eat peanuts, sunflower seeds, and suet.

Common Grackle. The grackle will eat anything—including mice, frogs, fish, and other birds—and is often considered a nuisance. They are especially fond of sunflower seeds and corn.

Pine Siskin. The pine siskin occasionally visits the United States from northern Canada; when it comes, it flocks to niger feeders.

Red-bellied Woodpecker. This woodpecker has a pale rosy belly and a bright red head. At the backyard feeder it enjoys suet, sunflower seeds, raisins, nutmeats, and rice. It is most common to the Southeast.

Hairy Woodpecker. This is the larger cousin of the downy woodpecker. It eats suet, peanuts, nutmeats, and cracked corn.

Red-breasted Nuthatch. This nuthatch is found in New England, the West, and northern Canada. It will sometimes store food in cracks and crevices of trees and houses. At the feeder, it eats suet, peanuts, nutmeats, and sunflower seeds.

Red-winged Blackbird. An occasional visitor to backyard feeders—where it looks for suet, seeds, and nutmeats—the red-winged blackbird will usually disppear as quickly as it appears.

Song Sparrow. Another popular backyard bird, the song sparrow often comes to feeders in the winter, looking for millet, canary seed, and finely cracked corn.

White-throated Sparrow. This sparrow's striking black and white striped crown make it easy to identify. At the feeder, they look for peanut hearts, hulled sunflower seed, canary seed, and millet. A shy species, it will leave when more aggressive birds arrive. It might pay to put some fine grains off to the side for this bird.

Purple Finch. Often confused with the house finch, the purple finch is a frequent visitor to the backyard feeder, where it searches for thistle, canary seed, and sunflower seed. It doesn't mind eating high above the ground, so it's a good bird to attract to second-story windows.

Northern Flicker. A member of the woodpecker family, the Northern flicker lives across the United States and parts of Canada. It occasionally visits feeders to eat suet.

American Crow. This omnivore occasionally visits backyard feeders to eat corn and suet.

Carolina Wren. This southeastern native sometimes visits backyard feeders to eat suet, or even peanuts and sunflower seeds.

Brown-headed Cowbird. Another not-so-favorite feeder bird, the cowbird usually arrives in a large flock that stays long enough to eat all the cracked corn that is available; then the birds look for sunflower seed, peanut hearts, and canary seed. They are usually raised by "foster families."

Red-winged Blackbird

Song Sparrow

White-throated Sparrow

Purple Finch

Northern Flicker

American Crow

Carolina Wren

Brown-Headed Cowbird

Common Redpoll

Carolina Chickadee

Common Redpole. A resident of Northern Canada, the redpole will occasionally visit feeders in the United States—usually in large flocks looking for hulled sunflower seed, canary seed, and thistle.

Carolina Chickadee. This cousin of the black-capped chickadee loves sunflower seed and suet.

Improving the Backyard Habitat

Birds are attracted to areas that have trees and shrubs that provide food, shelter, and nesting sites as well as an ample supply of water. The first step in improving your backyard habitat is to survey your yard or garden. Do you have small trees or seed-producing shrubs or bushes? Do you have nectar-rich flowers? Do you have areas where you can introduce flowers and plants that are important to birds? What improvements can you make to increase the availability of the necessities? Where can you introduce a feeder or source of water?

Food for birds can be provided by adding plants or a feeder. A well-placed feeder should fit into the natural habitat; it will attract more of the types of birds that are already in the region. The ideal location for your feeder is where you can see it from your home. It should be placed in the sun, out of the wind, and near sheltering trees or shrubs.

If your yard lacks shelter and nesting sites, you can add evergreen or deciduous trees, thick hedges, or shrubs. An alternate solution is to create a brush pile or hang birdhouses for nesting.

If you watch birds feeding, you will notice that they usually fly from a large tree to a smaller tree or shrub, then to the feeder, and back again. Take advantage of the birds' habits and place your feeder accordingly. If the area where you want to put your feeder doesn't have shelter nearby, you could plant a shrub, a berry-producing tree, or an evergreen near the feeding station. Over time, as these plantings mature, they will provide not only shelter but also natural beauty and abundant food.

Providing good habitat is the key to successfully attracting birds to your backyard. Improve the habitat, and the birds, and other animals, will come.

It's also important that a source of water be nearby. If your yard doesn't have a natural water source, such as a creek or pond, put up a birdbath. There's no better way to attract birds to your yard than by providing a year-round source of fresh water for bathing and drinking.

A bird must drink often to avoid dehydration, even though it gets some of its water from food. Bathing is also critical to birds. Feathers protect birds from rain, snow, heat, and cold; they are an important part of courtship; and they make it possible for birds to fly. Consequently, birds must keep their feathers in tip-top condition. They do this by bathing in water when it is available—even in winter—and in sand when it is not.

You can buy a birdbath—they come in a wide variety of sizes, shapes, and materials—or you can make one from a round, shallow dish. The dish should have a slightly rough surface; the material should not be slippery, as the birds must be able to maintain a good foothold while drinking or bathing.

In addition, your birdbath should provide a

gradual transition of water depth. This can be accomplished by using a sloping dish or by placing a small, flat rock at the edge. A gradual slope from a depth of one-half inch at the edge to about three inches at the center seems to work best. This gives the birds shallow water for bathing and deeper water for drinking.

Keep the bath clean and the water supply fresh. Place the birdbath a distance away from the feeder to prevent disease and near shelter to give birds protection from predators as they drink, bathe, and preen.

To make your yard even more attractive to birds, provide dripping water. You can puncture the bottom of a bucket, fill it, and hang it over the birdbath, or you can buy a commercial dripper or mister to attach to your hose outlet.

You will also attract more birds if you provide open water in winter, when other water sources are frozen. You can use an electrically operated submersible birdbath heater, or simply position the bath so that it gets direct sun to melt ice during the day.

Improving your backyard habitat combined with knowing specific habits of birds will help you create an environment that will attract an abundance of birds. The basic idea is to learn what a bird needs and then provide the real thing or a good substitute.

The Proper Feeder

The type of feeder you should use in your backyard depends on where the birds you want to attract feed naturally as well as on the types of food they eat. There are four broad categories of feeders: platforms, tubes, bottles, and baskets.

Commercial bird baths come in all shapes and sizes. Newer models recirculate the water to keep it fresh and clean.

Platform feeders, and box feeders with trays, are good for birds that normally feed on the ground, since the platform provides a flat surface for feeding that is similar to the ground. Platform feeders often attract a wide variety of birds, and you can usually fill them with inexpensive seed because most ground-feeding birds enjoy cracked corn or white proso millet.

A tube feeder is preferred by birds that feed in shrubs and bushes because the tube is like the stem of a shrub or the trunk of a bush. The feeder's perches simulate limbs or branches, and the seed ports simulate seed pods. Keep in mind that plants produce only one type of seed, so the tube feeder should be filled with only one kind of seed—sunflower seeds, peanuts, safflower seeds—not a mixture.

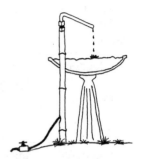

Nothing seems to attract birds better than dripping water.

Bottle feeders are ideal for nectar-eating birds, such as hummingbirds, which will sip sugar water from a tube as they do from flowers.

Basket feeders are used to hold suet, the best substitute for insects, the preferred food for birds that feed on tree trunks, such as woodpeckers.

Birds that eat fruits and berries require special attention. The feeder you use and where you place the food depends on the fruit or berry you are offering. Berries should be placed at shrub height; fruits should be placed a little higher, at tree height. I usually put fruits and berries on a peg or in a specially designed fruit feeder and hang it from a tree or pole. Birds prefer overripe fruit instead of fresh. Overripe bananas, apples, cherries, and grapes, as well as raisins will attract mockingbirds, catbirds, grosbeaks, and wrens. Orioles and tanagers like overripe oranges.

Choosing the Right Type of Feed and Feeder

Type	Represents	Preferred Food	Attracts
Platform feeder: Any flat surface House or box: Modified platform	The ground	Mixed seed: Similar to weed seeds found on the ground in an open area	All seed-eating birds and perching seed eaters
Tube feeder: Plastic or ceramic	Shrubs and bushes	One kind of seed: Usually sunflower, peanut hearts, thistle, or safflower	Chickadees, titmice, grosbeaks, grackles, finches, and others
Suet feeder: Coated wire or wire and wood	Insects and grubs	Suet cakes: Rendered	Woodpeckers, nuthatches, warblers, chickadees, titmice, thrashers, towhees blue jays, and others
Nectar feeder	Flowers	White sugar and water: Usually 1:4 ratio	Hummingbirds and orioles
Fruit feeders: Upright or platform	Berry bushes	Apples, oranges, currants, raisins, and other fruits and nutmeats	Robins, blue jays, grosbeaks, orioles, bluebirds, and others

Foods that Attract Birds

Once you decide which birds you want to
attract, determine that your yard has suitable
habitat for them, and choose a feeder, you need
to learn what and where they like to eat. The
best way to do this is to carefully observe how
birds eat in the wild. For example, watch tow-
hees and mourning doves and you'll notice
that they scratch and ruffle through debris on
the ground looking for weed seeds and small
insects. Goldfinches walk up and down golden-
rod and aster stems looking for seeds. Chickadees will carefully check each tiny branch of a
tree for insects and ripening seeds.

*A platform feeder can pro-
vide both seed and suet.*

Generally, backyard birds fall into four food
preference groups: seed eaters, insect eaters,
fruit and berry eaters, and nectar eaters. Most
seed-eating birds feed on the ground or at shrub
or tree height. Insect eaters feed primarily on
tree trunks. Fruit and berry eaters feed in the
branches of fruit trees and bushes. Nectar eaters
sip their sweet treat from tubelike flowers.

Seed-eating birds will eat a wide variety of
commercial feeds, with oil sunflower seed being
the most popular. Other choices include white
proso millet, peanut kernels, red millet, canary
seed, German millet, milo, wheat, cracked corn,
niger, hulled oats, buckwheat, rice, and rape
seed. You can buy all one type of food or mixes
that contain several varieties. Bird feed is regu-
lated by federal and state laws that require list-
ing ingredients in the order of their percentage
in the mix by weight. Each package must also
carry a nutritional analysis of the contents. This
is listed in terms of crude protein, crude fat, and
crude fiber and represents the overall nutrition

Where Birds Like to Eat

Bird	Ground	Shrub	Tree	Trunk
Blackbird	●			
Cardinal	●			
Chickadee	●	●	●	●
Doves	●			
House Finch	●	●	●	●
Goldfinch		●	●	
Grackle	●	●		
Grosbeak	●			
Jay	●	●	●	
Junco	●			
Mockingbird	●			
Nuthatch			●	●
Purple Finch	●	●	●	
Siskin		●		
Sparrows	●			
Titmice		●		
Woodpeckers				●

of the mix taken together. As a rule of thumb, the higher the proportion of protein and fat, the better the seed. Moisture is just that, the moisture content of the seed at the time of packaging. Seed should be relatively dry—about 13 percent moisture.

The accompanying chart will help you get started, but your best sources of information about which foods attract birds in your area are people who have been feeding birds for some time. They know what is best for your local environment and bird population.

Common Bird Feed Products
Following is a list of the most common bird feed products and a brief description of their benefits and the birds they attract.

Some commercially made feeders come with a feeder, a pole, and a baffle to keep out pests.

Black Oil Sunflower Seed. This is truly the most attractive seed to the widest variety of seed-eating birds. Research at the Cornell Laboratory of Ornithology shows that birds prefer black oil sunflower seed two to one over other sunflower seed varieties. Black oil seed should have been cleaned, recleaned, and de-sticked before it is packaged for sale.

Black-striped Sunflower Seed. This variety of sunflower seed is not nearly as popular as black oil seed, but larger seed-eating birds, especially grosbeaks and cardinals, enjoy it.

Niger Seed. Goldfinches, pine siskins, redpolls, house finches, and purple finches relish niger seed, also known as thistle seed. Niger seed is grown in Ethiopia and India and is sterilized in

Preferred Natural Food and Substitutes

Bird	Favorite Natural Food	Commercial Seed Substitute
Blackbird	Field grains	Corn
Cardinal	Fruit/Grains	Sunflower
Chickadee	Insects, seeds, and berries	Suet/Sunflower
Dove	Weed seeds	Mixed Seed
House Finch	Weed seeds	Niger
Goldfinch	Weed and tree seeds	Niger
Grackle	Omnivorus	Corn
Grosbeak	Tree seeds/Fruit	Sunflower
Jay	Acorns	Peanuts
Junco	Weed seeds	Mixed Seed
Mockingbird	Fruits	Dried Fruit
Nuthatch	Insects	Suet
Purple Finch	Weed seeds	Niger
Sisken	Weed seeds	Niger
Sparrow	Weed seeds	Mixed Seed
Titmice	Insects, nuts, and berries	Peanuts
Woodpeckers	Insects	Suet

USDA-supervised plants before it is sold in the United States.

Safflower Seed. This seed's claim to fame is that squirrels generally don't like it. It's a favorite of northern cardinals, mourning doves, and titmice. This pure-white seed is grown in the West and Midwest, especially in California and Arizona, and in Canada. Off coloring sometimes occurs when the growing season is wet; this has no effect on the seed's popularity with the birds.

White Proso Millet. White proso millet is primarily known as a seed for ground feeders. Birds from mourning doves to sparrows like it. It is the second most popular mixed seed ingredient, after black oil sunflower seeds.

Cracked Corn. Ground-feeding birds especially love cracked corn; other kinds of birds, including the northern cardinal, like it, too. The corn you buy for birdfeeding is usually steel cut and graded to medium size. Corn dust, or starch, is to be expected in bags that include cracked corn. (In the early spring, corn dust attracts honeybees.)

A tube feeder's tube represents the stem of a flower or the trunk of a shrub or tree; the perches represent limbs or branches.

Split Peanuts. This is a relatively new ingredient in feed formulations. It has replaced peanut hearts in many of the better mixes. Split peanuts are especially attractive to titmice, chickadees, blue jays, and white-throated sparrows.

Mixed Seed. Mixed seed usually contains some or all of the above seeds blended in different

Woodpeckers will eat suet as a substitute for their favorite food: insects.

percentages. Mixtures with the highest percentage of black oil sunflower seeds are the most popular, and usually the most expensive. Mixtures that don't include cracked corn are a good choice in the summer to discourage blackbirds.

It's fairly simple to attract birds to your backyard if you observe them in the wild and give them the food, water, and shelter they need. Next we'll learn how to design feeding stations to attract four popular birds—bluebirds, finches, hummingbirds, and woodpeckers. By following these examples, you should be able to attract any birds that inhabit or visit your area.

Bluebird Feeders

Bluebirds are usually ahead of the robins in their northward journey and arrive at my home in Pennsylvania amid the late winter storms of February. These colorful birds haunt open woods, fields, and orchards. They travel in groups of two, three, or four seeking food and nesting sites.

If you enjoy bluebirds as much as I do, you can set up a special feeder just for them. First, make sure that your area supports bluebirds. A call to your local Audubon Society, bird club, conservation office, nature center, or a bird-loving neighbor will answer this question.

To attract more bluebirds to your yard, tailor the habitat on your property to their needs. Keep in mind that bluebirds' feeding habits differ in summer and winter. To attract bluebirds in summer, when they eat mostly insects, set aside an area that has low-cut and varied vegetation. Bluebirds like to be able to see the ground in order to search for insects. While feeding they usually perch on low branches, keeping an eye on the ground below, and then drop down on unsuspecting insects. Bluebirds' favorite summer foods include grasshoppers, crickets, ground beetles, spiders, and caterpillars. If you don't have small trees or shrubs that provide the blue-

To attract bluebirds you need to provide a good habitat with short grass, open fields, berry bushes, perches, and suitable nesting sites.

birds a perch, add perches by attaching limbs to stakes driven in the ground.

Bluebirds can overwinter even in cold climates if there is a good supply of food, water, and shelter from the cold. The main winter foods of bluebirds are not insects, but berries from shrubs, trees, and vines. To improve your habitat for wintering bluebirds, begin by planting trees, shrubs, and bushes that hold their fruit into autumn and winter. These berry-producing plants are good bluebird foods:

Logs drilled out and filled with a bluebird suet mixture will attract bluebirds.

Bayberry *(Myrica caroliniensis)*
Black cherry *(Prunus serotina)*
Flowering dogwood *(Cornus florida)*
Hackberry *(Celtis occidentalis)*
Hawthorn *(Crataegus* spp.)
Holly *(Ilex* spp.)
Mountain ash *(Sorbus americana)*
Multiflora rose *(Rosa multiflora)*
Pyracantha *(Pyracantha* spp.)
Snowberry *(Symphoricarpos albus)*

When I was director of a nature center I had some success in getting bluebirds to feed on mealworms in the early spring and dogwood berries in the late fall. Bluebirds will eat suet products containing fruits and berries as well. You can also buy a commercial bluebird feed or make the following recipe: Start with two cups of a mixture of chopped raisins, currants, sunflower hearts, and berries. Next, add one-half cup solid vegetable shortening, one-half cup peanut butter, two cups cornmeal, and one cup flour. Blend thoroughly until dough is the consistency of putty. Form small balls or strips to use in your bluebird feeder. This mixture can be stored in the refrigerator for later use. Since bluebirds naturally feed on the ground, platform feeders work best. Over the past few years, there have been many attempts to get bluebirds to come to feeders designed especially for them. People have had success with trays filled with berries, raisins, and mealworms, and hollowed-out logs filled with a suet-berry mixture. Also, specially constructed bluebird box feeders have been shown to work very well, but they require a little patience.

My daughter and son-in-law put out a bluebird box feeder at their home in upstate New York and filled it with a commercial bluebird food. Bluebirds stayed at their farm until late December and then returned in February to use the nest boxes Barbara and Tom had put up.

The most popular bluebird feeder currently on the market is a box feeder with properly sized entrance holes in each end and clear sides to help the birds see the food; these are similar to the one Barbara and Tom used. These box-type feeders can be purchased at most hardware stores, garden centers, and wild bird specialty shops. If you'd like to build your own, refer to the accompanying diagram.

You may need to train bluebirds to use a box-type bluebird feeder. The best way to teach a bluebird to enter the hole to get food is to attach small sprigs of berries to the outside of the feeder next to the entrance hole. This, combined with a quality berry suet and some mealworms in the feeder, will usually entice the bluebirds to enter it.

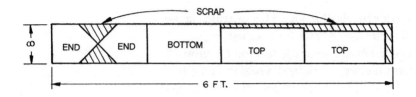

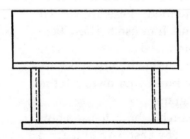

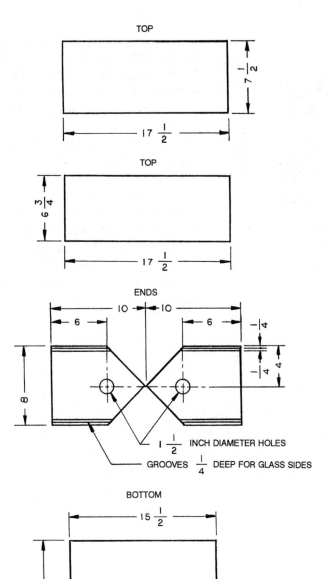

TOP

$7\frac{1}{2}$

$17\frac{1}{2}$

TOP

$6\frac{3}{4}$

$17\frac{1}{2}$

ENDS

10   10

6   6

$\frac{1}{4}$

8   4 $\frac{1}{4}$

$1\frac{1}{2}$ INCH DIAMETER HOLES

GROOVES $\frac{1}{4}$ DEEP FOR GLASS SIDES

BOTTOM

$15\frac{1}{2}$

8

ALL MEASUREMENTS INCHES
UNLESS OTHERWISE NOTED

Providing good habitat, nesting sites, water, and a reliable food source will help the popular bluebird thrive.

The bluebird is a beautiful bird. It is also beneficial because it eats destructive insects. Maintaining a year-round bluebird feeder will help the birds survive food shortages. Feeders are also helpful during nesting time, when demand for food is high. In northern areas where bluebirds are known to overwinter, feeders help to ensure the birds' survival during ice storms and cold spells, when berries are frozen in place. To help bluebirds even more, take special care to protect them from their natural enemies—cats, squirrels, and English sparrows—and make nesting boxes for them. If you provide good habitat, nesting sites, water, and a reliable food source, you can help the bluebird thrive.

Finch Feeders

Many kinds of finches will come to your yard or garden looking for small seeds and insects. Not all of them come every year, however. Many species live in Canada and come to the United States only every few years. Depending on where you live, you can look for purple finches, houses finches, Cassin's finches, American goldfinches, and lesser goldfinches every year. Pine siskins, grosbeaks, pine grosbeaks, crossbills, and redpoles come to the U.S. only when the Canadian winter is harsh and food supplies are scarce.

Finches are popular birds that are easy to attract to your yard or garden with a tube feeder designed especially for them and filled with niger seed, their favorite food. Niger is a tiny thistle seed *(Guizotia abyssinica)* grown mostly in Ethiopia and India for pressing into an inexpensive cooking oil. The niger seed that is shipped to the United States as bird feed is sterilized to prevent it and any associated weed seeds from germinating and becoming a pest.

Niger is a favorite food of American goldfinches, pine siskins, purple finches, house finches, and common redpolls. Other finch species, such as the lesser goldfinch, Lawrence

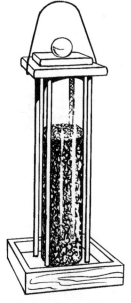

A commercially made vertical perch feeder is very popular with goldfinches.

A double vertical perch feeder offers twice as many feeding ports.

Some commercial feeders are specially designed to deter house finches from feeding at them.

goldfinch, hoary redpoll, rosy finch, and Cassin's finch may occasionally visit your yard, but they are not common feeder birds. Although related to finches, crossbills and grosbeaks prefer sunflower seeds and will probably not frequent your finch feeder.

A good finch feeder is a sturdy tube feeder with perches designed for finches, and a small hole made to dispense niger seed or tiny sunflower hearts. If you have ever watched goldfinches walking up and down the stem of an autumn aster, you will understand just how a vertical-perch finch feeder works.

Many backyard birders consider the house finch an unwelcome guest because there are so many of them and they tend to be aggressive toward their more popular cousins, the goldfinch, the pine siskin, and the redpoll. If you share this feeling, you can buy a commercial feeder designed especially to attract goldfinches and discourage house finches. One such feeder, the upside-down feeder, has several small seed-dispensing holes located under the perch. This is effective because goldfinches seem to have little trouble hanging upside down to feed, while house finches prefer standing upright. Another discriminatory finch feeder has shorter perches, which seem to discourage house finches while attracting other finch species.

Hummingbird Feeders

Nothing rivals the awesome wonder of the delicate, insectlike hummingbird. The hummingbird gets its name from the humming noise its rapidly moving wings make as they vibrate at a rate of fifty to two hundred times per second. Hummingbirds can hover over flowers and even fly backwards.

The hummingbird can be seen at least briefly each year from coast to coast; it may summer in your region or simply pass through during their spring and fall migrations. Of three hundred known species of hummingbirds worldwide, sixteen are found in North America. The ruby-throated hummingbird is the most common East Coast species, while the broad-tailed, black-chinned, and rufous hummingbirds are common in the West.

Hummingbirds feed primarily on the nectar found in tubular flowers. Therefore, the best way to entice hummingbirds into your yard is to plant a variety of tubular perennials or annuals. Hummingbirds will come to flowers in a porch, deck, or patio planter or to an entire section of the garden planted just for them.

It's a good idea to plant several different varieties of flowers that bloom at different times. This will keep the hummingbirds coming back

There are sixteen different types of hummingbirds in North America:
Anna's
Allen's
black-chinned
blue-throated
broad-billed
broad-tailed
buff-bellied
calliope
Costa's
Cuban emerald
lucifer
magnificent
ruby-throated
rufous
violet-crowned
white-eared

The delphinium is an excellent hummingbird flower; the hummingbirds eat nectar from the flowers. In the fall, goldfinches like to pick seeds from the stalks.

Scarlet sage, which flowers from July through October, is another hummingbird favorite.

and make your yard colorful throughout the summer. When planning your hummingbird garden, carefully consider the height of the plants (short in front to tall in back) to give the hummingbirds access to all of them. Also be sure to allow enough space between plants so the birds can feed comfortably.

Do not use any insecticides or other chemicals in your hummingbird garden. Harsh chemicals are harmful to hummingbirds, and small insects that live in the flowers add important nutrients to their diet.

Following is a partial list of recommended plants for the hummingbird garden. Select species that are orange or red, native to your geographic area, and have tubular flowers. These will be most attractive to hummingbirds.

Aloe (*Aloe* spp.)
Beebalm (*Monarda* spp.)
Begonia (*Begonia* spp.)
Butterfly weed (*Asclepias tuberosa*)
Cardinal flower (*Lobelia cardinalis*)
Columbine (*Aquilegia* spp.)
Dahlias (*Dahlia Merckii*)
Daylilies (*Hemerocallis* spp.)
Delphiniums (*Delphinium* spp.)
Fuchsias (*Fuchsia* spp.)
Gladiolus (*Gladiolus* spp.)
Honeysuckle (*Lonicera* spp.)
Indian paintbrush (*Castilleja* spp.)
Lupine (*Lupinus* spp.)
Nasturtium (*Tropaeolum majus*)
Petunias (*Petunia* spp.)
Red-hot-poker (*Kniphofia Uvaria*)
Scarlet sage (*Salvia splendens*)
Trumpet creeper (*Campsis radicans*)

Yucca (*Yucca* spp.)
Zinnias (*Zinnia* spp.)

Once you've enhanced the hummingbird habitat in your yard, the next step is to select a hummingbird feeder. Since hummingbirds are nectar eaters, you should use a bottle feeder filled with sugar water.

You will be filling and cleaning your hummingbird feeder often, so choose one that's easy to disassemble and clean. Start with a smaller feeder and wait until your hummingbird customers are regularly emptying it before switching to a larger feeder. This will ensure that your feeder solution will not sit too long and spoil. Plastic and glass feeders are available. Plastic doesn't break, but the glass type is sometimes easier to clean.

Some commercial hummingbird feeders can be hung from a pole or a tree or attached to a window.

Fill your feeder with artificial nectar made from a commercial mix or by combining one part sugar and four parts water, boiling for one to two minutes, and allowing to cool. Do not use honey, as it may develop botulism and make hummingbirds sick. Also, do not use artificial sweeteners, as they have no nutritional value. Some people dye the sugar-water mixture red, but I don't recommend it. After all, natural nectar is clear. If you are inclined, you can hang red streamers from the feeder to increase your chances of attracting hummingbirds.

It is very important that you keep your hummingbird feeder clean. Sugar water can ferment, allowing mold and bacteria to grow and making the birds sick. Be sure to clean the feeder and fill it with fresh nectar every two or three days. Simply discard any leftover nectar, wash the feeder

Commercial hummingbird nectar is usually made from sucrose, which makes an excellent hummingbird food.

thoroughly with warm soapy water, rinse it in a solution of one part household bleach to ten parts water, rinse the feeder again in clear water, dry it, and then refill it with fresh nectar. A fresh mixture is more attractive to hummingbirds, too, so you'll see more birds with a clean feeder as well.

In addition, you need to think about bees and ants, which love sugar water. The best way to keep these insects out of the feeder and prevent them from clogging its tubes is to use a bee guard or ant trap.

As with any birdfeeder, you should put your hummingbird feeder in a place that blends in with the landscape and allows you to see and enjoy the hummingbirds when they come. I suggest you put your hummingbird feeder among flowers and where it is sheltered from wind. If you live in a warm climate, place your hummingbird feeder in the shade. Since most hummingbird species are migrants, only visiting North America in warm weather, you should be sure to put your feeder up in time for the local hummingbirds' arrival. The timing of this will vary depending on where you live. It may be as late as April or May in the North and as early as January or February in the South.

So it's simple: Plant hummingbird flowers, put up a hummingbird feeder, provide fresh nectar, and then sit back and enjoy the birds. With a little effort your yard can become a hummingbird habitat, adding much beauty to the place where you live.

Hummingbirds flock to feeders after heavy thunderstorms. They have been known to stand on each other's backs to reach the feeder's nectar.

Woodpecker Feeders

In North America, we have a wide variety of woodpeckers, and most of them will come to your yard if you provide the right food and habitat. One of the best things you can do to make your yard more attractive to woodpeckers is to leave a few dead limbs on the trees or even a dead tree standing in your yard. This may not be attractive to you or to your neighbors, but the woodpeckers will love it. Dead tree limbs provide food, shelter, and nesting sites.

A wood and wire feeder is an effective way to provide suet to insect-eating birds.

Woodpeckers are insect-eating birds that are easy to attract with a suet feeder. Suet—the fat found around the organs of animals—is an excellent substitute for insects, insect eggs, and insect larvae and has become very popular as a year-round feeding supplement for birds. The best suet is the hard, firm fat found around the kidneys of beef cattle. In years past you could buy suet from any butcher shop, but because raw suet goes rancid in warm weather, it was used only in the winter months. Today most suet sold as bird food is rendered—melted down and purified so it resists spoiling.

Adding a suet feeder to your backyard feeding station will increase the number and variety of birds in your yard and garden. Woodpeckers, as well as chickadees, titmice, nuthatches, jays, starlings, and creepers, are particularly fond of suet.

Suet feeders come in two common types: the wire basket and the net bag. A suet basket may be simply made of plastic-covered wire formed into a small box or tube, or it may include wood to hold the wire or serve as rain protection. Suet nets are made from cotton, nylon, or plastic string woven into a bag. An onion bag also works well. The birds eat the suet while clinging to the strands of the basket or net.

Some suet feeders require birds to hang upside down to get at the food. This deters large birds such as starlings.

Hang the suet feeder near the end of a tree branch inside the "drip line." This way the suet will be shaded from summer heat but be exposed and easily seen by birds in the winter. Screw a small cup hook into the underside of the tree limb to suspend the feeder. This is better than hanging a wire or chain over the limb because wire or chain will cut the bark and prevent nutrients from reaching the end of the limb and cause it to die. A cup hook makes a very small hole and allows the bark to remain intact on the rest of the limb. Don't put your suet basket on the trunk of the tree, because if it melts, the suet will attract insects that will eventually bore into the tree bark and kill the tree.

Use pure suet and suet treats in the winter, suet doughs and suet delights in the summer.

If starlings, jays, and other large birds are a problem at your suet feeder, consider buying a model with a wooden or metal roof. This type of feeder requires the birds to hang upside down in order to eat the suet. Most big birds, especially starlings, will not use this type of feeder.

Sanitation and Storage

It is very important to keep your feeding station clean to protect birds from disease, and to store bird feed properly to guard it against spoilage and insect or rodent infestation. This is easy to do if you use a little common sense.

The disease most common at bird-feeding stations is so-called songbird fever, caused by the bacterium *Salmonella typhimurium*. It occurs every several years in the spring and summer and is spread among the bird population when birds eat seeds and drink water contaminated by the droppings of infected birds.

The best way to prevent these and other avian diseases is to keep your feeder and the surrounding area clean. Take your feeder down regularly, empty it, brush it out, wash it in soap and water, soak it in a solution of one part bleach to ten parts water for five minutes, and rinse it again in fresh water. Allow the feeder to dry well before refilling it.

Keep the ground around the feeder clean by raking seed hulls regularly—at least once a week during the summer, monthly in the winter. This is necessary for three reasons. First, the mixture of hulls and fecal droppings is an excellent breeding place for disease. Second, leftover seeds can attract rodents that otherwise would

Birdfeeding presents absolutely no health concerns for you or your family. Dirty feeding stations affect only birds.

be satisfied with raiding neighborhood trash cans. Third, seed hulls, especially sunflower hulls, contain a toxin that will kill the grass under the feeder and even prevent new grass from growing after the hulls are discarded.

As a further precaution against songbird fever, Steven Sibley of the Cornell Laboratory of Ornithology recommends not using solid-bottom tray feeders in the summer. Instead, use a cylinder or hopper feeder, where birds stand on perches and eat clean seed through the openings in the feeder. Also remember that birdbaths should not be placed too close to feeders, but be put off to the side where seed and bird feces are less likely to fall into and contaminate them.

Although some people clean the plastic parts of their feeders with dishwashing liquid and water, I find that the plastic gets dulled by this cleaning method.

Birds can also become ill if they eat moldy grain. Toxic strains of a mold called *Aflagillus flavus* produce harmful substances called aflatoxins that have been found to cause cancer in songbirds. Like many carcinogens, aflatoxins must be ingested in large quantities to cause cancer. Prevention is therefore very simple: If you see mold growing on your bird food, discard it.

You can prevent mold growth and other spoilage by keeping seed cool and dry. I recommend storing bird feed in a metal trash can with a tight lid. Plastic trash cans, although less expensive, don't hold up against gnawing mice, squirrels, and chipmunks. If you store plastic cans in the garage, you are likely to find holes in the bottoms of the cans and much of your seed eaten.

I don't recommend storing seed in the house, as you may attract mice or find yourself fighting the meal moth. This gray or white moth can infest your stored seed during the summer. Four moth species are commonly found in cereal grains and wild bird feed: Indian meal moth, almond moth, warehouse (cocoa) moth, and Mediterranean flour moth.

The moth lays an egg in the grain, and a larva develops and eats a small portion of grain. Following the larval stage, the insect goes into the pupal stage by weaving a web in the grain. From the pupa comes a small moth, which mates and starts the cycle anew.

You can control meal moths during the larval and pupal stages by putting a BioStrip pest strip at the bottom of the metal can where you store the feed. Place a piece of wood on top of the strip, then pour in the fed and put the lid on tightly. Replace the strip every three or four months.

The Mediterranean flour moth doesn't destroy clothes or rugs, but it might invade boxes of dry cereal.

If the moths have already hatched and are flying around the garage or house, there are some very effective and environmentally safe ways to eliminate them. One method is to use the SureFire Pantry Pest Trap, which contains a lure that attracts grain moths, flour moths, meal moths, and seed moths. These disposable traps capture these pests and keep them out of sight. The lure in these traps lasts up to sixteen weeks.

Another common insect pest is the weevil, which makes the holes often found in sunflower seeds. The hole is created by the larva of the weevil as it exits the seed. This damage happens in the field while the sunflower is growing.

If you open a sunflower seed with a hole, you will notice that about 10 percent of the kernel has been eaten away, usually on the end. By the time the sunflower is harvested, the larva is gone and 90 percent of the kernel is still there

for the birds. To eliminate the weevil larvae in the field and preserve the lost 10 percent of the kernel would create more ecological damage than it would be worth. Affected seeds are safe to feed birds; in fact, 3 percent weevil damage is acceptable even in sunflower seeds sold for human consumption.

If you follow these commonsense guidelines and keep your seed cool and dry and your feeding station clean, you can enjoy safe backyard birdfeeding for years to come.

If you use a trash can to store your seed make sure that it is clean and dry. Seed will quickly become moldy if it gets wet.

Squirrels and Other "Pests"

What is a birdfeeder pest?

At one time I thought I knew the answer to that question. But it didn't take me long to learn that the definition of a birdfeeder pest lies in the eye of the beholder.

Are squirrels a pest? I would say yes, but a lot of people spend a great deal of money feeding squirrels. I'm amazed by the number of squirrel feeders in the marketplace. I also know of two companies that subsist entirely on the sale of feeders and corn products especially for squirrels.

Are blackbirds a pest? Again, I always thought so, until I met a man who was upset because his neighbor had a black bird with a brown head at his feeder—a cowbird. He want me to tell him how to get some of those nice black birds to come to his feeder.

But back to the question. What do you do about those critters that come to your feeder that you regard as pests?

You can remove the pest from the area. If the pest is a mammal, use a live animal trap and relocate the creature a good distance from your home, preferably on the other side of a natural barrier, such as a river.

I have found that metal lever-activated feeders that close when a squirrel or heavy bird tries to feed are effective.

Squirrel-control powders mixed with seed can be an effective way to deter squirrels from feeding at a backyard feeder.

If you don't remove the pest, you can prevent its access to your feeder. In the case of squirrels, that means protecting the feeder from the top, bottom, and sides. I have found that a good overhead baffle takes care of the top. Nothing will protect your feeder from the sides except distance. Place the feeder six to eight feet from trees or other objects a squirrel could use as a jumping-off point. If you have a pole-mounted feeder, a good pole baffle is in order.

Metal, lever-activated feeders—the ones that close when a squirrel or heavy bird tries to feed—also work for me. I have heard, however, that a tandem of squirrels—one on the back and the other on the front—beat the system.

I have had good luck keeping large birds, such as grackles and pigeons, off a tube feeder by shortening the perches.

Still, your best option is probably to learn to live with the pests. Try setting up an auxiliary feeding station just for pests and stocking it with the foods they like. For example, starlings and sparrows are fond of stale bread and table scraps, and squirrels like corn and nutmeats. This should help preserve the birdfeeder for the birds you prefer.

People sometimes ask what to do if a hawk or owl begins to attack birds at the feeder. This is likely to happen when a large concentration of birds visits your feeder in harsh weather. The solution is to place your feeder five to eight feet from cover (trees and shrubs). Then healthy birds will have no problem getting to safety in time. Weak and injured birds will be culled from the population—this is nature's way, and you can do little to prevent it from happening.

I like to look at so-called pests like I look at weeds, as part of the natural order. A neighbor once reminded me, "If you're going to feed wildlife, you'd better be prepared to feed all the wildlife." She has a point. Also, she has no pests in her yard or weeds in her garden—everything is welcome and given a place to live.

Some people put out food especially for squirrels. Maybe they no longer consider the squirrels pests, or maybe they hope to keep the squirrels away from the birdfeeder.

Questions and Answers

Is it true that birds eat their own weight in food each day?

Experts tell us that many species of birds do eat at least half their weight in food daily, and some actually eat the equivalent of their own weight. In the summer a wren, sparrow, or chickadee might feed its young fifty, sixty, even seventy times in one hour. This is why many people like to feed the birds all summer; they also like to see parents bring their young to the feeder.

How important is grit to a bird's digestion?

Most experts agree that birds require some grit (bits of sand, shells, mortar, and so on) as an aid to digestion. The bird ingests the grit; it lodges in the bird's crop, where it helps grind the food. Grit also provides minerals. Birds can usually get all the grit they need naturally, but you can put out eggshells or sand when it is snowy or icy.

Put your feeder in the sun, out of the wind, and near shelter such as trees, shrubs, or bushes.

Do birds eat salt?

Studies show that grosbeaks, crossbills, and siskins need a little salt in their diets. They usually obtain it from natural foods or by drinking from tidal pools. Most birds do not want or need salt.

Is it true that peanut butter can stick to the roof of a bird's mouth and kill the animal?

Dr. Charles Smith from the Cornell Laboratory of Ornithology has tried to document this widely circulated rumor but has been unable to do so. If you can afford to feed peanut butter to the birds, do it. The birds love it.

The body of a bird is approximately 70 percent water.

Is it true that once you begin feeding birds in the winter you should not stop because the birds become dependent on the food supply?

If you do suddenly stop feeding the birds it could cause problems, but so many people feed birds nowadays that the birds can usually go elsewhere to find food. They will go to the feeder down the block or forage in the fields and woods or fly to the next town. If you are erratic in your feeding patterns, however, you won't attract many birds.

Can I use a feeder with metal perches in the winter?

A bird's feet do not contain sweat glands, so they won't stick to metal when the temperature is below freezing. A bird's tongue is coated with a material that is very similar to human fingernails, so it won't stick to cold metal either, the way a human's might.

Do birds put on extra feathers during the winter?

The American goldfinch has about one thousand more feathers in the winter than it does in the summer. This indicates that birds do put on extra feathers the same way we put on extra clothes.

Is there any kind of bird shelter I can put up in the winter?

You might be able to find a winter bird shelter in a store or you can build a shelter from wood. Make it about 15 to 18 inches long and 4 to 6 inches square with perches inside. It will be appreciated; severe winter storms can be brutal on birds.

What should I do if a bird flies into a picture window or sliding glass door and falls to the ground?

Don't touch the bird. Keep dogs and cats away from the area. If the bird is not fatally injured, it will regain its strength and fly away in a few minutes. Picking up a stunned bird can induce a rupture of blood vessels or heart failure.

Birds fly into windows for two reasons. They think their own reflection is another bird and attack it. Or they try to fly through what they perceive to be an open space. To prevent accidents you must disrupt the bird's sight pattern. Hang a few pieces of colored string in front of the window or put a picture or decal on the glass.

Has birdfeeding increased the range of some songbirds? Does this harm the birds?

It is true that some songbirds have increased their ranges over the past years. Experts don't know the exact cause of this. Indications are

By watching birds carefully and learning their feeding habits you can identify their preferred foods and feeding locations.

If you ask the right questions and get the right answers, you will attract the right birds to your backyard.

that it has to do with both planting and feeding. Most experts agree that feeding birds has minimal effect on overall bird populations.

Do birds store food for future use?

Jays have been known to hide food and no doubt come back later to eat it. The California woodpecker is sometimes called the "acorn woodpecker" because it drills holes in trees and stores acorns in them. Chickadees and nuthatches have also been known to store food. The longer you feed birds and the more you observe their behavior the more you will be amazed at what they do.

Learning More

There are many fine organizations from which you can learn more about birds. Ask your friends and neighbors to recommend a local group, or ask at your local birding store. Write to these organizations for more information.

Cornell Laboratory of Ornithology
159 Sapsucker Road
Ithaca, NY 14850

National Audubon Society
Membership Data Center
P.O. Box 52529
Boulder, CO 80322

American Birding Association
P.O. Box 6599 Dept. WB
Colorado Springs, CO 80934

North American Bluebird Society
Box 6295
Silver Spring, MD 20906

Purple Martin Conservation Association
Edinboro University of Pennsylvania
Edinboro, PA 16444